Make Way!

Make Way!

200 Years of American Women in Cartoons

Monika Franzen and Nancy Ethiel

CHICAGO REVIEW PRESS

Library of Congress Cataloging-in-Publication Data

Franzen, Monika.
  Make way!

    1. Women—Caricatures and cartoons. 2. American
wit and humor, Pictorial. I. Ethiel, Nancy.
II. Title.
NC1423.F73   1987   741.5'973   87-24913
  ISBN 1-556-52023-9 (pbk.)

All but three of the cartoons in this collection are drawn from the archives of Historical Pictures Service, Inc., 921 West Van Buren, Chicago, Illinois, 60607. Permissions to reprint are noted below.
  The cartoons on pages 37, 38, 39, 40, 41, 42, 44, 48, 49, 86, 87, 88, 89, 91, 97, 98-99, 113, 127, and 128 originally appeared in *Life* magazine and are reproduced with permission of Jones, Brakeley, Rockwell, Inc.
  The cartoon on page 45, courtesy of the *St. Louis Star*; on page 47, © with permission of the Chicago Sun-Times, Inc., 1987; on page 131, courtesy of J.N. Darling Papers, University of Iowa Libraries, Iowa City; on page 132, © with permission of the Chicago Sun-Times, Inc., 1987; on page 133, drawing by George Price, © 1951, 1979 The New Yorker Magazine, Inc.; on page 134, drawing by Booth, © 1970 The New Yorker Magazine, Inc.; on page 137, courtesy of the cartoonist, Kate Salley Palmer; on page 138, reprinted with special permission of King Features Syndicate, Inc.; on page 139, reprinted by permission of United Feature Syndicate, Inc.; on page 140, © 1983, Washington Post Writers Group, reprinted with permission; on page 141, reprinted by permission of United Feature Syndicate, Inc.; on page 142, reprinted by permission: Tribune Media Services; and on page 144, drawing by R. Chast, © 1987 The New Yorker Magazine, Inc. The cartoon on the back cover of this book, © 1983, Washington Post Writers Group, reprinted with permission.
  The following three cartoons were furnished and permission for use granted by the cartoonists: on page 135, courtesy of Betty Swords; on page 136, courtesy of Bülbül; and on page 143, courtesy of Nicole Hollander.

Published by Chicago Review Press Incorporated, 814 N. Franklin St.,
  Chicago, IL 60610

For our daughters and sons

Contents

I hate looking at those old cartoons. I'm fascinated too. I look at them like I looked at horror movies when I was a kid. I'm ready to cover my eyes at a moment's notice. I get this terrible feeling that we didn't make it. That we didn't get the vote. . . that we let the guys tell us it was unnatural, . . .that women were bullied and ridiculed into giving up the fight. . . then I see the cartoon that shows the Women's Suffrage Bill has been ratified in 34 states and we only need two more. Then I know we're going to make it, and I can relax my jaw muscles and enjoy the rest of the cartoons. This part of the story has a happy ending.

Nicole Hollander

Introduction

Her-story is not the same as his-story—as 200 years of cartoons about American women demonstrate. The pictures you will see are only a few of the great barrage, drawn mostly by men, that set out to humiliate, intimidate, and ridicule the women who came before us—women who gave us the breathing space in our personal and political lives to carry on their struggle for equality. Some of the cartoons are supportive—nice to know there have always been a few good men.

The earliest cartoons about America sprang from the conflicts that led up to the Revolution. Once the Revolution was won, white male political leaders wrote themselves one wonderful constitution and announced the beginning of the Republic. Some women requested, quietly, that the men also "remember the ladies," but no dice. It wasn't until the next wave of political upheaval in the mid-nineteenth century that women, this time many more of them, brought the topic up again. This time they were not so quiet about it, but spoke out publicly at meetings of their own. And this time, cartoonists, now a flourishing species with hardly a female among them, took notice.

What they noticed was the beginning of the Women's Rights Movement. Women had joined anti-slavery organizations in the early nineteenth century. They were finally allowed to speak in public, proving to be passionate and able orators. They worked hard in various reform movements alongside reform-minded men. The reform-minded men liked that. Then women started talking about women's rights in addition to the abolition agenda. The reform-minded men did not like

1

that. After years of experiencing discrimination within the reform organizations for which they worked, women activists decided to work for themselves and started their own movement.

In 1848, in Seneca Falls, New York, Elizabeth Cady Stanton and other early feminists organized a convention to discuss "the social, civil, and religious rights of women," including the vote. They didn't stop in Seneca Falls, but held similar meetings in a series of states during the next decade. The meetings were greeted with a flood of hostility and derision by the press, and often with threats of violence by spectators inside and outside the meeting places. Yet women carried on, advocating such rights as the control of their own earnings and the right to keep their children after divorce (most states deeded both rights to husbands). And, to safeguard women's rights politically, the right to vote.

The Civil War (1861–1865) brought a halt to this first stage of the Women's Movement. National concerns and individual energies became focused instead on the war and the issue of slavery. Women's organizations addressed themselves to freeing the slaves, always with the hope that elective franchise for black men would also include the vote for black and white women. No such luck. With the war over and the slaves freed, women were admonished to remember that this was "the Negro's hour"—male only. Women of any color need not apply.

But activist women did not go away. In 1868, the women's suffrage amendment was first introduced in Congress, where it ebbed and flowed for five decades. A resurgence of suffrage organizations gathered force for a second stage of the Women's Movement in the 1890s. At the same time, women's interests expanded into founding organizations for the improvement of housing and education for the poor. Much of this activity was tolerated by men; it seemed close enough to the nurturing they expected from women, despite there being an uneasy political edge to it.

The beginning of the twentieth century saw more women in the work force than ever. Men were nervously guarding their fantasy of Victorian tradition, separating the ladies from the factory girls. It didn't work. Women from both factory and parlor organized unions, marches, and legislative petitions. Their leaders and organizations disagreed, overlapped, or presented united fronts, but eventually women did succeed in getting the vote in a few states.

Once again, a national emergency threw the Women's Movement off course. World War I cleared the home front of men, and women were needed to fill the positions vacated by the men at war. The need for women as workers lessened men's political hostility, and, seeing an opportunity, women stepped up their lobbying efforts for the vote. Finally, after much political wrangling, women won "the sacred right to vote" nationally in 1920. The Nineteenth Amendment was passed not necessarily because the men in power suddenly decided giving women the vote was a wonderful idea, but because those men needed women's votes (naturally, they presumed appreciation) to stay in power. In the end, the rationale was less important than the reality. Women had taken a big step, though far from the last step, on their long climb toward equal rights. New generations of women would take it from there.

With the vote in hand, women began to channel their energies in a number of different directions. Radical feminists believed that the vote alone was not enough and continued to work for an equal rights amendment to the Constitution. Sometimes they disagreed with advocates of working women, who believed in the necessity of protective labor legislation, and with feminists working for social reform that included child labor laws. All this activity made women a recognized political and social force in their first decade of suffrage.

Then came the Depression. Through that great economic upheaval and the slow recovery that followed, it appeared to many that the fire that had burned in women during more than a century of struggle had been extinguished. Then, beginning with World War II, women accelerated their movement into the labor force, and the 1950s saw more married women enter the working world than any other decade. But these were invisible facts, routinely obscured by the fifties fantasy of the happy homemaker and the dizzy blond—favorites of strip cartoonists across America. Rarely did women figure as the subjects of political cartoons.

When the Women's Movement regrouped in the 1970s, its agenda was strikingly similar to the demands women had made a century before. Cartoonists, now largely more sympathetic (and more of them female), often reflected on the persistence of women's fight for equal rights—a fight that is yet to be won. The 1912 cover cartoon by Laura Foster, one of the few female cartoonists of that period, remains relevant; women continue to cry, "Make Way!"

Woman as Symbol

"'We, the people of the United States.' Which 'We, the people'? The women were not included."

Lucy Stone

Early in American history, women appeared only as symbols in cartoons, a role that would gradually recede in later centuries. One of the earliest of these representations, a sixteenth-century engraving of a Native American woman, sums up the view of Indians as bloody savages—and of the untamed woman as an enormous threat to men.

When Europeans started to invade the North American continent seriously during the seventeenth century, they brought the feisty art of satirical drawing with them. It was a handy political tool, employed during the Revolutionary War and other tense political moments. Women were often central to the visual concept, though only as symbols for some nation or other. Later, they would also get to star as symbols for peace, justice, and prosperity, often coyly wrapped in yards and yards of gossamer or clad in flowing Roman tunics, showing lots of shoulder. Real women, meanwhile, were up to their necks in the muck of survival before, during, and after the Revolutionary War. Not until the nineteenth century, when their struggle for equal rights begins to heat up, do women appear in cartoons in their own right.

5

America by Philippe Galle, 1581

Anonymous, Revolutionary War, 1776

Anonymous, Revolutionary War, 1782

9

THE SHADOW OF ENGLISH LIBERTY IN AMERICA

Anonymous, 1850

World War I recruiting poster

The Early Struggle for Equal Rights

"The true republic—men, their rights and nothing
more; women, their rights and nothing less."

Susan B. Anthony

The overwhelming majority of cartoonists, especially in the early years,
were men. And their cartoons have generally reflected not women's
view of themselves, but men's view of women—a view much affected
by the feelings, both positive and negative, that women evoke in men.
Rarely did early cartoonists concern themselves with women's own
feelings and desires—especially for equality. They were far more con-
cerned with the threat these desires posed to their own comfortable
way of life.

Nineteenth-century cartoonists gleefully included white and
black women active in the abolitionist movement in withering anti-
abolitionist caricatures, then moved full speed from there to lam-
pooning the first few women's groups that decided the time had come
to propose some freedoms and rights of their own.

The early cartoons were quite nasty. Then, somewhere near the
beginning of the fight for women's votes, a split seems to have occurred
among cartoonists. As women pushed for suffrage, cartoons ridiculing
the early women's organizations such as Sorosis (where intellectual
women met for "united thought and action") gave way to cartoons

depicting women as full of longing and hope for a different, more equal world for themselves and their daughters. Some cartoonists had lovely fantasies of the effects of women's essential purity harnessed to the power of the vote: America would be swept clean of evil and corruption once women could vote. It didn't happen.

Sympathy and hostility came in waves. Some cartoonists predicted that women would be just like men—tempted by and often succumbing to the lure of power and success. Or that women were simply too frivolous to be responsible voters. Some even expressed dread that the movement for rights would push men off their power base and into nothingness—as in the cover cartoon. Yet later, as women struggled closer to getting the vote, an encouraging number of cartoons again cheered them on—and were sweetly congratulatory when the Nineteenth Amendment finally passed in 1920.

ABOLITION TRACKS.

[*LATEST EDITION.*]

CAN'T FIND A REST FOR DE SOLE OB DE FOOT ARUM,
FY-YI-YI, GOT TO SHIN ALONG-ARUM,
BOYS FROW CAT-ARUM, PELT US WID DE EGG-ARUM;
FY-YI-YI, ALL'S GOIN' WRONG-ARUM!

Vanity Fair, 1861

THE AGE OF BRASS

Currier & Ives, 1869

WOULD-BE VOTERS
A Bevy of Strong-Minded Amazons Make a Sensation
at a New York Uptown Polling Place

The National Police Gazette, circa 1869

SOROSIS, 1869

Harper's Weekly, 1869

Entered, according to Act of Congress, in the year 1869, by D. APPLETON & CO., in the Clerk's Office of the District Court of the United States for the Southern District of New York.

SATURDAY, AUGUST 14, 1869.

"WILL SHE VOTE?"

Appleton's Journal, 1869

AN INAUGURATION OF THE FUTURE

Life, 1897

Cosmopolitan, 1899

AN UNEXPECTED EFFECT

Life, 1905

"AND NOW IS THE·WINTER OF OUR DISCONTENT."— *Richard III.*

Life, 1908

THE SPIRIT OF '09

Life, 1909

COMING

Life, 1910

THE TEMPTATION

Life, 1911

THE DREAM   AND   THE REALITY

Life, 1912

"I FEEL TWO NATURES STRUGGLING WITHIN ME"

Life, 1912

THE RENEGADE

Life, 1912

"MAKE WAY!"

Life, 1912

HER FIRST VOTE

Harper's Weekly, 1912

PURIFYING POLITICS
Will she be able to put any white spots on him?

Life, 1912

THE ONE WHO VOTES

Life, 1913

"Theirs not to reason why,
Theirs but to do and die."

Life, 1913

THE MINIMUM WAGE
Has she earned it?

Life, 1913

BARRED OUT
When woman has her vote

Life, 1913

THE OBVIOUS THING

Columbia: Oh, thank you so much, Uncle Sam.
I never doubted your gentlemanly instincts.

Life, 1913

Suffragette: I WONDER WHICH ONE WILL BE PRESIDENT?

Life, 1913

"—DREAMING DREAMS NO MORTAL
EVER DARED TO DREAM BEFORE"

Life, 1914

HUGGING A DELUSION

Life, 1915

poster, 1915

The 1920 Girl: I WONDER IF HE IS AFTER ME OR MY VOTE?

Life, 1920

THE LAST FEW BUTTONS ARE ALWAYS THE HARDEST.

St. Louis Star, 1920

Current History, 1920

NEARLY UP

Chicago Daily News, 1920

1776–RETOUCHING AN OLD MASTERPIECE–1915

Life, 1915

"CONGRATULATIONS"

Life, 1920

Fears About Equality

"Man is not the enemy here, but the fellow victim."

Betty Friedan

The prospect of women with the vote—however charming "giving" them the vote might be in theory—aroused massive male fears. Most of these revolved around the notion that the result would be role reversal, with women taking on the worst, most aggressive traits of men and men becoming passive wimps, ripe for exploitation by women. Cartoonists seemed unconscious of the irony implicit in portraying many female roles as subservient and onerous—a fact not exactly news to feminists then and now.

Sexual attraction unchecked by traditional roles was portrayed as a very dangerous business. More often than not, however, this was not likely to become a problem because liberated women were portrayed as unattractive, overbearing gorgons, mad with lust for power. On the other hand, the beautiful Victoria Woodhull didn't fare much better. The first woman to declare herself a presidential candidate, Woodhull held rousing speeches in favor of free love, and just generally seemed to have had a whole lot of fun. The result: a savage caricature of her as the devil's own mate, rejected and despised by "real" women.

Ranking right up there with men's horror of sexually aggressive women was their nightmare of getting stuck at home with the kids while women left for destinations unknown.

Meetings, perhaps? Carousing in bars? Who could be sure? Little did men know that someday they would actually want to spend time with their children—some men in fact, some in theory.

To get out of the house was not easy for women. It required economic wherewithal. It required being paid for their work. When women finally did gain some economic means—beginning with World War I while the men were far off fighting—cartoonists were quick to note that they might not want to give it up once the war was over.

Occasionally, women's own fears were expressed in cartoons. In 1912, Laura Foster summed up the dilemma of the woman who desires a career—can she succeed at work and still have love and marriage and children? The question Foster raised early in the century continues to torture women—and to obsess the media—today.

A GREAT NUISANCE

Dashing young lady: *"Will you allow me, Sir, the honor of escorting you home?"*
Modest young gentleman: *"I thank you Miss. I will not trouble you.*
Mamma promised to send the carriage for me."

Harpers Weekly, 1852

WOMAN'S RIGHTS

Dissipated Bloomer. "My charming Charles, don't be alarmed—is there anything so dreadful in the first kiss of a virtuous affection?"

The Lantern, 1852

THE FEMALE GENIUS

"The celebrated Mrs. M. E. Southworth Braddon Cobb, engaged in
writing her last new sensation novel, to contain 25 elopements, 43
separations from 'bed and board,' and 742 divorces for neglect,
abandonment, etc., etc., etc."

Yankee Notions, 1866

HOW IT WOULD BE, IF SOME LADIES HAD THEIR OWN WAY.

Harper's Weekly, 1868

Currier & Ives, 1869

Old Gent. "As Mrs. Nettlerash has gone to the Sorosis Club, I tho't I'd just come over with my Knitting. Baby not well, eh?

Young Gent. "No, poor thing, he requires so much Care that I really don't get time to do my Mending!"

Harper's Weekly, 1869

"WHO CAN LONGER DOUBT THAT
WOMAN RULES THE WORLD?"

Lady (*Member of the Woman's Rights Society, to Stage Driver*). "What do you mean by Starting before I've assisted my Husband out? Dear me! what can you expect of a Man?"

Harper's Weekly, 1869

WOMAN ASSERTS HER RIGHTS.

Punchinello, 1870

THE WEDDING RING,
As Sorosis would like to see it worn.

Punchinello, 1870

THE WIFE AND MOTHER AT A PRIMARY,

1872

"GET THEE BEHIND ME, (MRS.) SATAN"
Wife (with heavy burden). *"I'd rather travel the hardest path of matrimony
than follow your footsteps."*

A caricature of Victoria Woodhull, *Harper's Weekly,* 1872

A WOMAN'S RIGHTS.

1872

Mrs. Belva Lockwood, a prominent woman lawyer, ran for President on an Equal Rights ticket in 1884. The men of Rahway, New Jersey, tried to ridicule her by parading in Mother Hubbard outfits with striped stockings. Everyone laughed at the men instead.

1884

THE FEMALE RIGHTS' MUSKETEERS.
What may be expected if the schemes of certain strong-minded women
in America are realized.

The National Police Gazette, circa 1893

WOMAN'S RIGHTS.
Polite Conductor. *Excuse me,
Madam, but this car is the smoker.*

Aunt Polly Wanta. *I know it is,
young man. That's the reason I got in ter it.
Kin I trouble yo' fer a match?*

Puck's Library, 1893

NOWADAYS.
"My dear Susan, I wish you would keep your trowsers on your own side of the closet."

Life, 1895

WE ARE GETTING THERE FAST.
Stern Parent: *"Willy, isn't that Miss Bloomers going soon?*
—it's nearly eleven o'clock."
Son: *"Yes, Mama: she's just saying good night!"*

Puck, 1895

IN A TWENTIETH CENTURY CLUB.
"Why don't you fetch your brother here some night?"
"Oh, I think it's a bad atmosphere for a young man who has been
carefully brought up."

Life, 1895

THE COMING GIRL.
"Woman is every day enlarging her sphere."

Life, 1895

THE NEW NAVY.
ABOUT 1900, A.D.

Life, 1896

THE BLOOMER GIRL'S WEDDING.

Life, 1896

CONVENTION OF THE HUSBAND REFORM CLUB.
Subject for discussion at this meeting:
—How to make the home more attractive.

Life, 1896

THE COMING MAN.
"Tell her I'll be right down."

Life, 1896

IS THIS TO BE THE BALD-HEADED ROW OF THE FUTURE?

Life, 1897

THE AMERICAN SUFFRAGETTES

Harper's Weekly, 1907

THE DECLARATION OF INDEPENDENCE, 1909.

Life, 1909

Hotel Clerk: WE DO NOT RECEIVE MEN
UNACCOMPANIED BY A LADY.

Life, 1910

"DON'T THINK THAT BECAUSE THEY HAVE NO ESCORT
YOU CAN BE BRUTAL TO THESE YOUNG MEN, OR YOU'LL
HAVE ME TO DEAL WITH."

Life, 1910

WHEN WOMEN VOTE
The eleven gentlemen and one lady, having failed to reach a verdict,
are to pass the night in the jurors' room

Life, 1910

"NOT GUILTY"—ON ACCOUNT OF HIS GOOD LOOKS

Harper's Weekly, 1910

SOME AMERICAN HUSBANDS

Life, 1911

MERE MAN AND THE SUFFRAGETTE

DRAWN BY E. W. KEMBLE

Harper's Weekly, 1912

84

The Husbandette: Madam, you said you attended a political meeting last night. How do you account for this photograph of a horrid chorus boy which I find in your clothes?

Life, 1912

"OH, JOHN, FOR HEAVEN'S SAKE, STOP THAT BLUBBERING
ABOUT GOING HOME TO YOUR MOTHER! I'M SICK OF IT!"

Life, 1913

TAKING DOWN THE BARRIERS
Are equal rights really desirable?

Life, 1913

ADVICE TO HUSBANDS OF FEMINISTS
Beware of young and handsome stenographers

Life, 1914

1950 B.C.   1950 A.D.

MATING

Life, 1916

Private Brown—"*Who's been here while I've been away?*"

Literary Digest, 1919

She: I DON'T KNOW WHETHER I WANT TO GO BACK OR NOT

Life, 1919

LOOKING BACKWARD

Life, 1912

A Woman's Place

"A woman's place in society marks the level of civilization."

Elizabeth Cady Stanton

Equal rights petitioners, the sexually aggressive, and women involved in such suspect activities as Mormonism, temperance, and work for pay were obvious targets for cartoonists. But even the women who stayed home and did their best to fit into the little boxes of their prescribed roles were considered fair game. Mainstream topics like family and fashion were a frequent subject for cartoons, with courtship and marriage especially fertile ground. Woman starred in all her most glorious anti-male roles: the heartless temptress, the manipulative husband hunter, the ruthless social climber, the self-centered and financially irresponsible object of men's helpless attraction. Occasionally, a cartoon appeared on the enslavement that traditional marriage could mean for women, but this was rare.

When it came to fashion, ridicule of women who dared to be nonconformist and sensible, choosing to wear bloomers, was clear and blunt. Similarly enthusiastic ridicule was aimed at women who were not sensible enough and were mindlessly obsessed with fashion. Apparently there was a fine line in there somewhere that women had to identify and walk in order to appeal rather than appall.

Mormon women living in their polygamous Utah society fascinated cartoonists, who often expressed fears of the power these women, among the first in the nation to get the vote, could wield for their church. Cartoonists were more comfortable with the topic of poverty, with illustrations of good women struggling to save their children or of dying women whose children hoped to save them. This was one sure way for women to get social approval—by being good and dead.

Very lively, on the other hand, were the women who led the temperance movement. Initially, they were depicted sympathetically, as pure and angelic saviors of home and society. Then some of the organizations sullied themselves by affiliating with the suffrage movement. Cartoonists immediately stripped these sinners of their angelic status and transformed them into nasty little fanatics.

When wars were brewing or in full swing and men were in the army, the navy, or the air force, women entered the work force. And when they did, working women, whether professional or blue collar, were depicted with amusement or as charming (though probably rather inept) substitutes for men—a temporary situation, surely.

This gathering of Ladies (bless 'em!) is not caused by some one having
fallen in a fit, nor has a robbery been committed; it is merely a social
group discussing how a certain New Hat ought to be Trimmed.

Harpers Weekly, 1873

THE BLOOMER COSTUME.

A female, says one of our contemporaries, never appears so well as when attired in a simple dress. No artist ever decks his angels with towering feathers and gaudy jewelry; and our dear human angels, if they would make good their title to that name, should carefully avoid ornaments, which more properly belong to Indian squaws and African princesses. Those tinselries may serve to give effect on the stage or on the ball-room floor, but in daily life there is no substitute for the charm of simplicity. The engraving which we give herewith, our artist has represented from life, it being a picture of a lady who passed by our office up Tremont Street last week, and represents her dress precisely as she wore it. It was a regular "Bloomer," and created not a little surprise and excitement among the lookers on. In anticipation of the general adoption of this mode of dress, we see that a New York house has recently transmitted an order to Paris for an invoice of dress goods, with a deep border on the side. These goods are intended for ladies' short dresses, and the width of the cloth will comprise the length of the skirts. We give the following description from a New York paper:—"The skirt comes a little below the knee, and buttons in front; the waist is cut plain, and also buttons in front. The border extends round the skirt, and in front to the bottom of the waist—the latter being cut to have the border form the letter V. The trousers are made loose, gathered into a band at the ankle." This will prove a change of dress, indeed, but we do not look to see it generally adopted, by any means. The press have encouraged it because it is so bold and laughable; public taste will soon condemn it, however.

NAPOLEON.

His progress was a voyage through blood, toward mildness, peace, and justice. But in that ocean of blood there lay an island, and in the island did that perilous voyage terminate, and to it was our daring hero chained, till his soul departed. Against *one* island had this continental genius bent all the fury and the energy of his nature, and in *another* island was he for a time imprisoned, and in a *third* island he breathed his last.—*Gilfillan.*

TRUE MERIT.

Ease in your mien, and sweetness in your face,
You speak a syren, and you move a grace;
Nor time shall urge these beauties to decay,
While virtue gives what years shall steal away.
Tickell.

THE NEW FEMALE COSTUME.

Gleason's Pictorial Drawing Room Companion, 1851

FASHION

Life, 1913

Summer
Fashions

It will be interesting to see how many of the feminine graces
the truckwomen will retain

Chic but inexpensive little tub-frock
for street wear

Of course, some of the new
letter-carriers will refuse to wear
the old bull-dog shoes affected by
the extinct males

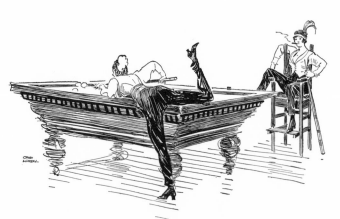

With trousers will naturally come much freedom of movement
hitherto denied

for Women

With the advent of trousers women will *really* smoke

If the new police-women refuse to wear trousers, then the skirts must be slit rather further up—otherwise all the thieves and aigrette hunters will get away

For the fire-lassies the rubber skirts will be made quite short, to permit of their jumping about, ladder-scaling, etc.

Life, 1914

Major Bayonet, of the Mormon Irregulars, consents, in a rash
moment, to give each of his devoted Wives a Lock of his Hair.
The result is very painful to behold.

Harper's Weekly, 1858

FEMALE SUFFRAGE.

Wouldn't it put just a little too much power into the hands
of Brigham Young, and his tribe?

1869

FRANK LESLIE'S ILLUSTRATED NEWSPAPER

Entered according to Act of Congress, in the year 1882, by Mrs. FRANK LESLIE, in the Office of the Librarian of Congress at Washington.—Entered at the Post Office, New York, N.Y., as Second-class Matter.

No. 1,376.—VOL. LIII.　　　NEW YORK—FOR THE WEEK ENDING FEBRUARY 4, 1882.　　　[PRICE 10 CENTS. $4.00 YEARLY. 13 WEEKS, $1.00.]

MORMONISM IN UTAH—THE CAVE OF DESPAIR.

IN THE BITTER COLD.

Harper's Weekly, 1858

"She must be getting better. It is the first time she
has smiled."

Life, 1894

JEWELS AMONG SWINE

Harper's Weekly, 1874

THE SENTINEL—TAKING DOWN NAMES
AT A DRINKING SALOON.

Harper's Weekly, 1874

Graphic, 1874

"Woman's Holy War: Grand Charge on the Enemy's Works," 1874

Currier & Ives, 1874

NEW YEAR'S
Guarding Against the Dangers of the Wilderness (1681),
and of Civilization (1881)

Harper's Weekly, 1881

The Mill and the Still

Harper's Weekly, 1883

THE SERPENT OF THE STILL

Harper's Weekly, 1887

A caricature of Carry A. Nation, U.S. Temperance Agitator,
Saturday Globe, 1901

"WINE, WOMAN AND SONG"

Life, 1919

THE WEDDING RING AGAIN.

Punchinello, 1870

IS THIS "WOMAN'S SPHERE"?

1896   115

COOL

Kate: *"They draft the single men first, Charlie."*
Charlie: *"Yes, I think they do, Kate. Why?"*
Kate: *"Nothing, only I was thinking how you could avoid the draft—that's all."*

Yankee Notions, 1862

THE COMING CAMPAIGN—
MAMMA MARSHALLING HER FORCES.

Frank Leslie's Comic Almanac for 1866

"WHY NOT?"

Why can't the Ladies belonging to the different Colleges have a
Regatta of their own next year? Let the First Prize be a husband with a
fortune, and we think the Winning Boat will make the
Quickest Time on Record.

Harper's Weekly, 1873

118

Harper's Weekly, 1875

A TENDER HEART.

He: I have three thousand a year. You could certainly live on that.
She: Yes, but I should hate to see *you* starve.

Life, 1890

WHAT LOVE AND A WOMAN CAN MAKE OF A MAN

Life, 1892

Rescuer: Miss Properleigh, give me your hand.
Drowning Maiden (preparing to sink for the third time): Oh, Mr. Manley;
this is so sudden! So unexpected! You will have to ask mamma.

Life, 1892

THE START

THE FIRST LAP   THE SECOND LAP

THE HOME STRETCH   THE FINISH

THE HUMAN RACE
from a woman's point of view

Life, 1912

LADY PRACTICE IN PHYSIC.

Mr. Smithers being sick, sends for a Lady Doctress to
attend upon him professionally. Being a singularly
bashful young man, Mr. Smithers' pulse is greatly
accelerated on being manipulated by the delicate fingers
of the Lady Practitioner, whereupon she naturally
imagines him to be in a high fever, and incontinently
physics him for the same.

Harper's New Monthly Magazine, 1853

GOV. MORTON LEADING ON HIS GALLANT
LAWRENCEBURG (IND.) BRIGADE.

"Now we feel it an everlasting disgrace that our bridges should be guarded by
Ohio soldiers when we have so many able-bodied men who should be formed
into regiments and prepared for duty. And we most earnestly request you to
take some steps to arouse their dormant energies and compel them to act as
men, or let us take their places, leaving them to attend to domestic affairs,
while we shoulder the guns you so generously sent here, and go forth to assist
you in protecting our homes."

—*Letter from the Ladies of Lawrenceburg to Gov. Morton, of Ohio.*

Vanity Fair, 1861

IN THE TOILS OF THE POLICE

Life, 1911

"GIRLS, THEY'RE GOING TO DEMOBILIZE US, AND WE'VE
GOT TO GO BACK TO WEARING PETTICOATS
AND TRYING TO BE EFFEMINATE."

Life, 1919

THE GIRL WHO USED TO DRIVE A NAIL WITH HER HAIR BRUSH

Life, 1919

The More Things Change . . . .

"Don't agonize. Organize."

Florynce Kennedy

Women won the vote in 1920. For the next fifty years, they did the best they could to further their cause—considering what war and the Great Depression dragged into the house. It took half a century for women to join forces and gather their strength for a third stage of the Women's Movement.

Women had seized the opportunity to work during World War II, and many had refused to go back home when the men returned, in spite of some very forceful propaganda. Laws, attitudes, and social mores still shackled many women into stifling lives, overused at home, underpaid at the office.

Then came the Civil Rights Movement of the 1960s. Women of all ages and from all backgrounds gave years—some, their lives— to this movement. Yet as women of all colors fought to make civil rights a reality for blacks, many of them were shocked into a rude awakening by the discrimination they experienced from men who could handle only one civil rights concept at a time.

Once again women upped and poured their energies into women's rights. They marched, wrote letters, gave time, gave money, wrote books, sued employers. They insisted that women's studies become a recognized discipline in the white male halls of academe. Some chose to stay home with their children and teach them that girls can be astronauts and presidents and that it's OK for boys to cry. Others divorced, decided against marriage, decided to love women, or decided to wait and see. Women fought for jobs on construction crews and as firefighters; they fought very hard and came a very long way.

But not all the way. Most eyes are still on women when it comes time to make coffee. But, hey, what's another fifty years among friends?

LETTING THE GENIE OUT OF THE BOTTLE

The Des Moines Register & Tribune, 1943

Costume Jewelry

Chicago Sun-Times, 1950

The New Yorker, 1951

"I've got an idea for a story: Gus and Ethel live on Long Island, on the
North Shore. He works sixteen hours a day writing fiction. Ethel never
goes out, never does anything except fix Gus sandwiches, and in the end
she becomes a nympho-lesbo-killer-whore. Here's your sandwich."

The New Yorker, 1970

134

"THIS IS OUR EXPERIMENTAL PHYSICS LABORATORY, THIS IS OUR X-007 DATA PROCESSING CENTER, AND THIS IS OUR WOMAN."

M.C.P. Calendar, 1974

San Francisco Examiner, 1979

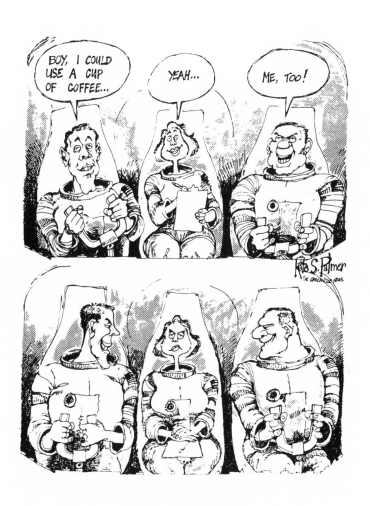

The Greenville News, 1977

The Charlotte Observer, 1982

LOOK GUYS... WHY DON'T WE JUST SAY THAT ALL MEN ARE CREATED EQUAL... AND LET THE LITTLE LADIES LOOK OUT FOR THEMSELVES?

The Dayton Daily News, 1982

The Philadelphia Inquirer, 1983

Atlanta Journal, 1982

Chicago Tribune, 1984

SYLVIA

by Nicole Hollander

1985

The New Yorker, 1987

Acknowledgments

My heartfelt thanks go to: Patricia Herminghouse, who way back when and singlehandedly plucked me out of undergrad confusion and dropped me into grad school; to Bill Matheson, who made me want to stay there; to Libby McGreevy, for seeing a book when all I showed her was one cartoon; to Amy Teschner, an astute and supportive editor—a wonderful experience for a first-time author; to my husband, Laurens V. Ackerman and my son, Marcus Kabel, for their devoted typing and enthusiastic encouragement; to my daughter, Alexandria Kabel, and my son, Sean Franzen Ackerman, for believing in me as a matter of course; to Lynn Weiner, for setting me straight—repeatedly—on Feminist Studies; to Mariel Burch and Kate Bishop, who shared ideas and insights while running up enormous phone bills; to Durrett Wagner for critical conversations and positive feedback ever since I arrived on these shores "at the tender age of. . ."; to Janet Ohlhausen—14 years of friendship and enlightened insistence on the real meaning of life: fun; to my group: Shirley Cristol, Myra Ducharme, Marylou Gadin, Carolyn Jacobs, Edith Kravitz, Corey Mostow, Kathy Pratt, and Janet Schroeder for their steadfast listening skills and sisterly support; to my father, Henning Franzen, for doing the best he could in a difficult world; and to my mother, Irma Franzen, who made life possible, day by day from 1940 to 1945, when life was seriously impossible.

Monika Franzen

About the Authors

Monika Franzen has her Ph.D. in German Literature from Washington University in St. Louis. She is a freelance writer and photographer, a staff writer for *Chicago Parent News Magazine*, part owner of Historical Pictures Service, Inc., in Chicago, and an activist for feminist causes.

Nancy Ethiel is a freelance editor and writer for a number of national magazines and newsletters, as well as the author of several books on health education and travel. Her interest in feminism was first aroused while serving as a Peace Corps volunteer in Kenya, where male volunteers were issued motorcycles and female volunteers were forbidden to ride on them. She subsequently became a founding member of the Evanston Women's Liberation Center in Evanston, Illinois.